Houseplants for All Seasons

By Anne Halpin

Neil Soderstrom, Principal Photographer

Published by:
TYPHOON MEDIA CORPORATION

Houseplants for All Seasons

Houseplants for All Seasons

Publisher
Simon St. John Bailey

Editor-in-chief
Elaine Evans

Producer, Editor and Principal Photographer
Neil Soderstrom

Prepress
Precision Prep & Press

Photography
All photos by Neil Soderstrom except following:
- Alan and Linda Detrick: 40left, 47
- Creative Homeowner's *Complete Houseplants* by Jack Kramer, photos by David Van Zanten: 5bot rt, 6Bamboo-Chinese-Corn, 17, 18top, 19, 20, 21, 24bot, 26left, 27, 28, 30, 31left, 32top, 33top, 34, 35, 38top, 42, 44, 45, 49left, 51left, 52, 53, 55bot, 56, 57bot, 61
- Garden Picture Library: 7 by Mayer/Le Scanff, 8top by Steven Wooster
- istockphoto.com: 4–5top3, 6Dragon, 10top, 32left, 63
- LeeValley.com: 9

ISBN 9781600814440
UPC 615269144411

2010

Printed in the United States

Houseplants for All Seasons

Part 1: Caring for Houseplants

Sharing Your Home with Plants 4-6
What Plants Need 7
Light 8-9
Potting Mixes 10-11
Feeding Your Plants 12-13
Watering 14-15
Care through the Year 16-17
Making More Plants 18-21
Helpful Tools 22
Pest and Disease Control 23

Part 2: Best Houseplants

African Violet 24-25
Anthurium 26
Balfour Aralia 27
Cacti 28-29
Chinese Evergreen 30
Dumbcane 31
Dracaena 32-33
Ferns 34-35
Fig 36
Fittonia 37
Gold Dust Plant 38
Guzmania 39
Ivy 40
Jade Plant 41
Moth Orchid 42-43
Palms 44-45
Peace Lily 46
Peperomia 47
Philodendron 48
Polka Dot Plant 49
Pothos 50
Prayer Plant 51
Purple Passion 52
Rubber Plant 53
Snake Plant 54-55
Spider Plant 56-57
Ti Plant 58
Umbrella Plant 59
Wax Plant 62-63
Index 64

Part I
Sharing Your Home with Plants

It's good to have plants in your home. Plants bring a little bit of nature indoors. We don't all live in the country surrounded by flowers and trees. But we can all get up-close and personal with plants.

You don't need a sunny window to have houseplants, as long as you can give them a little light. If you haven't got a window, grow plants under fluorescent lights. Here I'll tell you everything you'll need to take care of more than 40 of the most popular types of houseplants.

Where to Put Them

Houseplants can transform your décor. In a contemporary home, plants can soften sharp lines and hard surfaces. In a more casual setting, they add color, texture, and charm.

A large plant like a rubber plant or a palm can decorate a room like a piece of sculpture. Low plants can bring color and structure to a table or countertop. You can group plants on windowsills, plant stands, and occasional tables. Use them on a table in an entryway. Set a plant on the landing of a bright staircase. Fill a kitchen window with plants.

Caring for Houseplants

Houseplants vary widely in the kinds of care they need. Some can get by with an occasional watering, while others need soil that is constantly moist. Some houseplants like a sunny window while others need soft, filtered light.

If you give your houseplants growing conditions that are similar to the natural environments their ancestors once came from, they will flourish.

Peace lily

Outdoor sliding glass doors are an ideal light source for plants. If you position different shapes and sizes in front of one of the doors, they'll look like spring even when the snow flies outside.

Fun with Plants

If you have kids, plants can be fun. When your cactus blooms, it's an event. When the spider plant makes babies, it can be a game to see how many you get.
Then you can put each baby in its own little pot and give them as gifts. It's a lesson in life.

Houseplants that Purify the Air

These air-purifying plants are also among the toughest houseplants you can grow. Taking care of plants is healing. Plants are good for the body as well as the mind. In the 1980s NASA researchers found that some plants have the ability to remove toxins such as benzene, formaldehyde, and trichloroethylene from the air. And many of the most effective air-purifying plants are common, everyday houseplants.

These plants are survivors. They will grow without sun, and they won't keel over if you forget to water them. Although they can withstand some neglect, remember that they're living things. You do need to give them a reasonable amount of light and water, and feed them once in a while. But they're pretty forgiving.

Bamboo palm
Chinese evergreen
Corn plant (Dracaena)
Dragon tree (Dracaena)
English ivy
Golden pothos
Peace lily
Philodendron
Snake plant

What Plants Need

Houseplants tend to like the same room temperatures that we do, though some like it on the cool side and others like it warmer. As in nature, many plants like it cooler at night, so turning your thermostat down 5 or 10 degrees at night will make your plants happy while saving on your heating bills.

Indoors we can control the environment to a great degree. Humidity is the most difficult aspect to manage, especially in winter when central heating turns our homes into mini deserts. But there are ways to boost humidity, too.

Plants need five basic things in order to grow:

- Light
- Moisture
- Humidity
- Nourishment
- Favorable temperature

Understanding Plant Growth

Most plants go into dormancy–or rest–for part of the year. When a plant rests, it stops blooming and producing new leaves and shoots, and its color may look a bit faded. During this period, reduce watering so the soil is just barely moist, and do not fertilize. When you see signs of new growth, gradually increase watering and resume feeding.

Light

All plants need light to grow, but some need more than others. The brightest, strongest light and the most direct sunlight comes in a south-facing window. South light is too strong for some plants, and they may sunburn. Cacti and many flowering plants love a south window, but it can be too much for many foliage plants.

TIP

Too much light: If you notice a plant's leaves developing brown-and-crispy or pale and washed-out zones, it may be getting too much light.

An east window receives morning sun, and a west window receives afternoon sun; the rest of the day these windows get bright light but no direct sun (this is considered moderate light). Many foliage plants, and a host of flowering ones, too, like an east or west window.

A north window is dimmest, admitting no direct sun but staying softly lit all day. In this low-light environment many ferns and foliage plants thrive, including peace lily and philodendron.

I like to soften the sunlight entering the south windows of my living room with lace curtains (you can use sheers, too). In a dim north window, you can increase light a windowsill plant receives by placing a light-colored "bounce panel" between the plant and the room.

Using Electric Lights

If you don't have good windows for plants, you can grow them under electric lights. Although you can buy special "grow lights" or expensive mercury vapor lights, full-spectrum fluorescent tubes or a combination of warm white and cool white tubes work just fine.

Lights on!

Keep fluorescent lights on 12 to 14 hours a day for foliage plants, and 14 to18 hours a day for flowering plants.

Too little light

When plants don't get enough light, their stems bend toward the light, the stems elongate, and leaves grow farther apart. If this happens, turn the plant around and either move it closer to the light source or find a brighter spot for it.

For plants to get enough light from electric lamps, the fixtures must be just a few inches above the tops of the plants.

(Floralight photo courtesy of LeeValley.com)

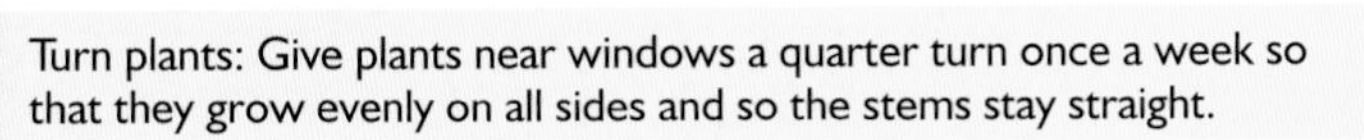

Turn plants: Give plants near windows a quarter turn once a week so that they grow evenly on all sides and so the stems stay straight.

Potting Mixes

Houseplants don't generally grow well in garden soil. Outdoor soils are too heavy for indoor potted plants and can contain disease-causing organisms or other pathogens. But a light, loose potting mix that combines soil with a few other ingredients will ensure that houseplant roots get plenty of air.

When soil is soggy all the time, plant roots are unable to take in oxygen and the plant eventually suffocates. Peat-based potting mixes are lightweight and easy to use, but if you are concerned about depleting the world's finite supplies of peat, grow your plants in a medium lightened with coir fiber or perlite instead.

There are lots of good packaged potting mixes on the market. Some contain fertilizers and others do not. Fertilizer-containing mixes are convenient, but I think doing your own fertilizing allows you better control. You can, for instance, stop feeding plants when they go into a rest period. If you use a packaged potting mix, make sure it is a potting *mix* and not just potting *soil*, which by itself is too heavy and dense for most plants. Look at the ingredients on the bag if you're in doubt.

It's also easy to make your own potting mix (see the recipes next page). Most plants like to be repotted into fresh soil every year or so. For big plants that would be difficult to repot, I just scrape the top couple of inches of soil out of the pot and replace it with fresh potting mix.

Pots may be glazed or unglazed pottery, unglazed terra-cotta, plastic, metal, or woven wood lined with plastic containers.

(Examples courtesy of Hollandia Nursery, Garden & Patio, Bethel, CT)

Potting Mix Recipes

Mix ingredients thoroughly when making potting mixes. Moisten potting mixes before planting.

All-Purpose Potting Mix

1 part potting soil or garden loam
1 part finely crumbled compost or leaf mold
1 part sharp (builder's—not beach) sand or vermiculite

Soilless All-Purpose Potting Mix

1 part peat moss
1 part perlite
1 part vermiculite

Humusy, Well-Drained Mix

1 part potting soil
1 part fine grade fir bark

Cactus Mix #1

1 part potting soil
1 part sharp sand

Rich Mix for Humus Lovers

1 part potting soil
2 parts crumbled compost
1 part sharp (builder's) sand or perlite

Cactus Mix #2

1 part potting soil
1 part sharp sand
1 part compost
½ part small pebbles or fine gravel

Feeding Your Plants

Plant roots absorb nutrients from soil, and you need to fertilize to keep the plants supplied with nutrients. Fertilizers may be solid (molded into spikes or beads or tablets), granular, powdered, or liquid, synthetic or organic.

Fertilizer types: sticks, beige scratch-in granules, blue concentrated crystals, garden compost, brown fish emulsion, and green liquid concentrate.

Fertilizer Types

Liquid fertilizers: concentrated and must be mixed with water for use. Can be messy, but easy to dilute to a milder strength if desired.

Granular fertilizers: need to be scratched lightly into the soil surface. Best for large plants in big pots; can be hard to handle in small pots.

Plant food spikes and tablets: easy to handle, but dosage rates are a bit uncertain.

Fertilizer beads: easy to scatter over the soil surface, but don't completely dissolve and are always visible.

Organic fertilizers are natural materials that are mild and slower acting. Synthetic fertilizers are fast acting and stronger, so you use less of them. Their downside is that if you apply too much of them, they can burn plant roots.

Water well after applying granular or solid fertilizers.

Understanding Fertilizer Labels

Whatever type of fertilizer you choose for your houseplants, it's important to provide the right balance of nutrients (a balanced diet). Plants need three major nutrients:

Nitrogen (N) promotes healthy leaves

Phosphorus (P) supports root growth and ripening of seeds and fruit (and therefore flower production)

Potassium (K) helps fruit formation, photosynthesis, and uptake of other nutrients.

Foliage plants like these variegated umbrella plants need plenty of nitrogen fertilizer, and flowering plants need more phosphorus.

An all-purpose plant food that contains all three major nutrients works well for a wide variety of plants and is generally your best choice. Or, choose an organic product that also includes minor and trace elements. Follow package directions for application rates, though as I've qualified below.

When to Fertilize

Plants need fertilizer most when

- They are actively growing, producing new leaves and stems
- They are setting buds and blooming

Young plants need less fertilizer—or none at all—when they're resting (dormant). You don't eat when you're sleeping, and plants don't either.

Also, watch your plants and get to know them, and you will soon learn their behaviors.

HELPFUL TIP

A simple feeding option: You can give plants a little food every time you water them so you don't have to remember when it's time to fertilize. For this, use a liquid fertilizer diluted to 1/2 or 1/4 the strength recommended on the package.

Watering

Confused about how much and how often to water your houseplants? Don't worry, you're not alone. In fact, the biggest cause of houseplant demise is overwatering. Follow these simple guidelines and you won't go wrong.

- Learn what the plant needs—some like even moisture, others need to dry out between waterings.
- Water thoroughly. Excess water will drain from the hole in the pot's bottom when soil is wet through. Pour off excess water remaining after 15 minutes so roots don't become waterlogged.
- Plants in small pots need water more often than plants in big pots (smaller volume of soil holds less).
- Plants in clay pots need water more often than plants in plastic or glazed ceramic pots (moisture evaporates through the porous walls of unglazed clay pots).
- Plants growing, budding, or blooming need more water than resting plants.
- Thin-leaved plants dry out faster than plants with thick, fleshy leaves.
- Plants in warm rooms need watering more often than plants in cool rooms.

Rule of thumb for watering: I poke my finger into the pot. If the soil feels dry an inch below the surface, for most plants it's time to water. Cacti and dormant plants are exceptions.

Water houseplants from the top, pouring water onto the soil, or from the bottom, by pouring water into the saucer underneath the pot (when soil surface feels moist the soil is wet through).

Humidity

Plants need humidity in the air around them as well as moisture for their roots. Some need more humidity than others. Cacti and other succulent plants can do with a lot less.

How to boost humidity for plants that need it

Fill a clean spray bottle with water and then thoroughly mist the plants. Once a day is enough for some. Others need misting two or three times daily.

To increase humidity around plants, I like to set their pots on pebble trays. This is simply a layer of pebbles in the bottom of a shallow tray with water filled to its rim. Set the pots on the pebbles, and add water when the level drops.

HELPFUL TIP

If your bathroom has a bright window or a skylight, it's a perfect place for a couple of plants. They'll love the humidity and will soften the look of tile, chrome and porcelain. Hanging baskets won't take up floor space.

Care through the Year

Here are some other things your plants are going to need from time to time.

Grooming

To keep plants looking good, pinch off flowers as they fade and dry. Also, pick off any damaged or browning leaves. If the plants look dusty, wipe large leaves gently with a damp cloth. To remove dust from smaller-leaved plants, set them in the sink and mist them or rinse with a gentle spray of tepid water.

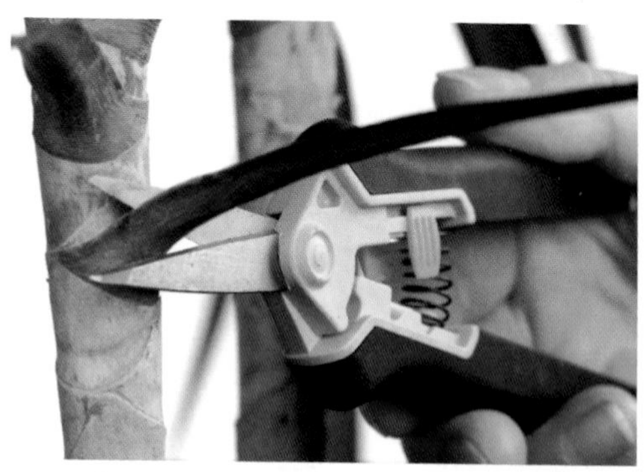

Pruning can improve shape and keep plants bushy.

Repotting

When a plant's roots fill the pot, move it to a bigger one. Many plants don't grow well in a pot that's too big for them. So even though it's tempting to move it to a pot several sizes bigger, it's better to move up just one size.

The best time to repot most plants is in spring when they are growing actively. Examine your plants to see if they are potbound (meaning the plant's roots completely fill the soil in the pot—you may even see roots growing out of the drainage hole in the bottom). Some plants actually like to be crowded in their pots and some bloom better this way. But many like some room to grow.

How to repot a plant

First, plan ahead. Water the plant a few days before you plan to repot. If you're going to use a clay pot, soak the new pot in water overnight before repotting.

Cover your work surface with newspaper. Remove the plant from the old pot.

If the plant doesn't slide out easily, run a knife around the inside to loosen the root ball.

For a large plant, run a long knife or a ruler around the inside of the pot to loosen the plant. Lay the pot on its side and slide out the plant.

Cover the drainage hole in the new pot with a piece of cheesecloth or paper towel to keep soil from washing out when you water.

Your goal should be that the top of the root ball be at the same height it was in the old pot. To test this, add a layer of moistened potting mix to the pot. Then set the root ball in the pot to check the height. If the plant is too low, add more potting mix and then recheck the height. If it's too high, remove some potting mix.

When the plant is at the right height, fill in around the sides with potting mix. Water to settle the soil. Then add more if needed.

1. After removing plant from pot, scraping away old soil, and cutting off dead, brown roots, gently untangle remaining roots.

2. After placing some potting mix in bottom of new pot, set the plant in. Then fill in with potting mix around the roots and fill to within ½ inch of top of pot. Shake gently to settle soil.

3. Water well, and add more potting mix if necessary. After 15 minutes, dump any water that remains in the drainage saucer.

Making More Plants

Starting new plants from old ones is called propagation. Here's what to do.

Stem Tip Cuttings

Cut off the top 6 to 9 inches of a healthy stem. Cut just below a leaf node (small bump on stem from which a new leaf will grow). Remove lower leaves and dip end of stem into rooting hormone powder. Insert stem 2 inches into a pot of moist growing mix.

To maintain humidity, place a clear plastic bag over the pot, holding it off the cutting with dowels. Keep out of sun. Water when the medium is dry. When you pull gently on the cutting and feel resistance, roots have formed. Plant the new plant in its own pot.

Keep the medium evenly moist and be patient, checking periodically to see if your cutting has rooted.

Stem Cuttings

For large plants with thick, cane-like stems, such as this dracaena stem, try stem cuttings. Remove a healthy stem and cut it into pieces a few inches long. Look for scars on the pieces where leaves used to be, and make sure any cuttings you plant have a leaf scar—that's where new leaves and shoots will grow. Remove any leaves and smaller stems from the cutting. Dip cutting in rooting hormone powder and plant it horizontally an inch or so deep in moist, sterile growing medium.

Finger tip points to leaf scar.

Dividing Plants

When a plant forms a clump with multiple stems, split the clump into two or more new plants. Unpot the plant and cut through the root ball with a sharp knife, so that each division has stems and roots. Replant the divisions in moist potting mix.

Dividing Offsets

Some plants form offsets at their base that look like baby plants. Carefully sever the offsets from the parent plant with a sharp knife and replant them in new pots of moist potting mix.

Air Layering

If an old plant, such as a rubber plant shown here, has developed a long, woody stem over time, you can propagate by air layering.

With a sharp knife, make a diagonal cut partway through the main stem, a few inches above the soil. Place a toothpick in the cut to hold it open. Moisten some unmilled sphagnum moss and wrap it around the stem to cover the cut. Holding the moss in place, wrap with a piece of clear plastic and tie or tape that shut at top and bottom with string or electrical tape.

When you see roots growing in the moss underneath the plastic, cut off stem at its base. Be patient! It can take six months or more for roots to form. Remove the plastic and plant the rooted stem in its own new pot.

After removing lower leaves, cut diagonally partway into stem.

Insert toothpick into the cut, made just below a leaf node.

After wrapping cut tightly with sphagnum moss, enclose tightly in plastic tied at both ends.

You can find care instructions for this rubber plant (*Ficus*) on page 53.

Helpful Tools

To take good care of your houseplants you'll need a few basic tools:

Manicure scissors—for tiny nips

Sharp knife—for pruning and taking cuttings

Flower shears or scissors—to cut back thinner, softer stems and remove spent flowers

Pruning shears—for pruning branches and stems of large or woody plants

Old kitchen spoon and fork—for loosening soil and a zillion other uses

Trowel—for lifting plants out of pots, blending potting mixes, and scooping potting mix.

Gloves—gardening gloves to keep hands clean, and heavy-duty leather ones to handle spiny cactus

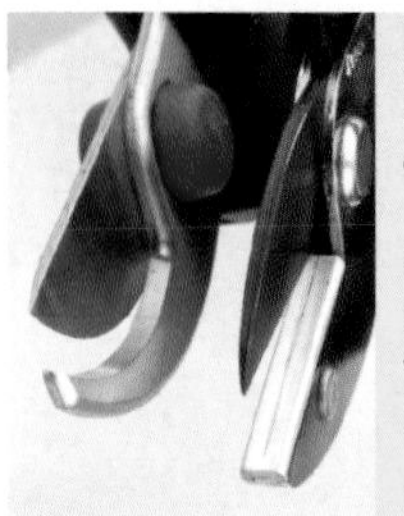

Left: Bypass pruners cut cleanly.

Right: Anvil-type pruners tend to crush stems, if not kept sharp.

Watering can—one with a long spout

Mister—a used spray bottle, thoroughly cleaned, works just fine for misting plants

Pebble tray—for boosting humidity.

Pots—Clay pots are versatile, and there are all sorts of colorful, decorative containers to complement your décor. For trailing plants you'll need hanging baskets and hooks or brackets to hang them from.

Stakes and supports—tall plants and slender stems may need staking. Use thin wooden dowels, slender bamboo canes, or sturdier stakes as needed. A metal rod with a looped end works great for orchids. A slab of tree bark can support philodendrons and other climbers.

Pest and Disease Control

If you keep your houseplants in good condition and provide the growing environment they need, they'll be unlikely to develop problems. Yet, sometimes pests or diseases can attack despite your best efforts. The best defense is a good offense so keep a close eye on your plants. Monitor leaves (undersides too!), stems, the axils where leaves join stems, and the soil surface for signs of trouble. Take action as soon as you notice problems.

If trouble strikes, use the least toxic measures first. To get rid of small pests, dip plants in mild soapy water, followed by a thorough rinsing in lukewarm water. But for mealybugs (white cottony masses in leaf axils), dab each with a cotton swab dipped in rubbing alcohol. Insecticidal soap is effective against a wide range of pests, and horticultural oil sprays are useful on scale and spider mites. Always follow package directions when using any pest or disease control products, and never spray indoors. Take plants outside to treat them.

TIP

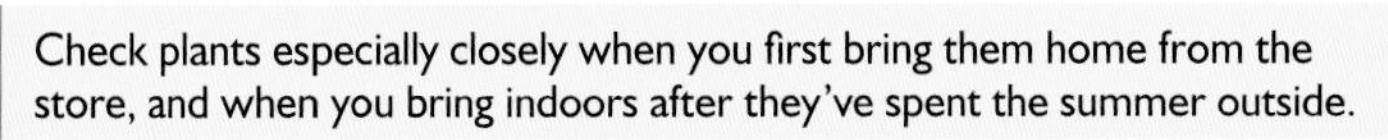
Check plants especially closely when you first bring them home from the store, and when you bring indoors after they've spent the summer outside.

Part 2: Best Houseplants

Here's a quick guide to growing lots of great houseplants. For details on potting mixes, boosting humidity, and other techniques, see pages 7–23.

African violets (*Saintpaulia*)

African violet (*Saintpaulia*)

These much-loved plants are easy to care for, take up little space, and bloom throughout much of the year. The plants produce a low rosette (clump) of glossy, deep green, rounded to oval to heart-shaped leaves with a hairy surface. There are also trailing varieties and miniatures. Clusters of five-petaled flowers appear year-round when the plants receive sufficient light.

Flowers may be single or double (with twice as many petals), pink, deep red, purple, blue, white, or bicolored, with smooth, ruffled, or fringed edges. Picotee flowers are edged in a second color.

Potting Mix: Equal parts milled sphagnum peat moss, perlite, and vermiculite.

Temperature: 65 to 75°F year-round.

Light: Moderate to bright light from east or west window, filtered by sheer curtains. No direct sun.

Moisture: Let soil surface dry between waterings; do not overwater. Use lukewarm water. Ideal humidity level is 60 to 70%, but adapts to lower humidity in bright light.

Fertilizing: Feed monthly with all-purpose fertilizer or biweekly with half-strength liquid fertilizer.

Other Care: Likes consistent conditions all year. Blooms best when pot-bound; transplant only when roots completely fill the pot. Turn often so plants grow evenly. Start new plants from leaf cuttings (see Snake Plant page 55).

When an older plant develops a "neck"—an elongated stem—rejuvenate it to improve its looks. Remove plant from pot and with a sharp knife scrape stem just below the bottom leaves to expose the green tissue beneath the outer surface. Remove soil from around root ball, and cut off bottom of root system.

Repot plant in fresh, moist potting mix, deep enough to bury scraped part of stem. Enclose the potted plant in a clear plastic bag for a month, until it grows new roots. Check often to be sure soil is moist but not wet. Open bag occasionally to let in fresh air. Remove bag when roots have formed (a gentle tug on the plant will meet with resistance).

Multi-plant moisture tent

Anthurium (*Anthurium*)

Also called flamingo flower and tail flower, anthurium is a tropical plant from Central and South American jungles. It has heart-shaped deep green leaves. The long-lasting exotic-looking flowers may be red, white, coral or pink. They consist of a single hood-shaped spathe wrapped around a columnar spadix (the "tail").

Potting Mix: Equal parts potting soil and fine-grade fir bark; good drainage is important.

Temperature: Prefers warm temperatures of 70° to 85°F. Keep out of cold drafts.

Light: Bright to moderate light, ideally from an east window, with some direct sun in winter.

Moisture: Keep soil evenly moist. Prefers high humidity; mist twice a day, place on a pebble tray, run a humidifier nearby, or keep in a brightly lit bathroom.

Fertilizing: Feed every 2 to 4 weeks with mild all-purpose fertilizer.

Other Care: Repot when roots fill most of the pot space. Start new plants by division (page 19).

INTERESTING FACT

A relative of anthurium, *Amorphophallus titanium*, has a 12-foot-tall flower that smells like rotting meat!

Balfour Aralia *(Polyscias)*

This attractive upright foliage plant can grow to about 4 feet high indoors, or taller over many years. It has small rounded leaves with irregular edges. One variety, 'Marginata,' has grayish green leaves edged in cream. Over time, stems grow woody and the plant takes on the look of a small tree.

Potting Mix: All-purpose potting mix

Temperature: Range from 65 to 80°F; lower temperatures can cause leaf drop.

Light: Bright, direct light from an eastern or western window, with some direct sun.

Moisture: Does not like soggy soil. Let soil dry to about an inch below the surface; then water well. Empty any water that has drained into the saucer under the pot 15 minutes after watering—don't let the plant sit in water. Generally not finicky about humidity.

Fertilizing: Feed monthly when growing actively, with all-purpose fertilizer. Fertilize less during winter.

Other care: If plant grows too tall, prune stem tips to maintain a more manageable size. Clean leaves occasionally with a damp cloth. Repot when roots fill most of the pot space. Start new plants from stem tip cuttings in spring (page 18).

INTERESTING FACT

Balfour aralia has an interesting family tree. It's in the same botanical family as English ivy, umbrella plant, and ginseng.

Cacti   Crown plant (*Rebutia hybrid*)

Cacti — Old man cactus (*Cephalocereus senilis*)

Cacti and other so-called succulent plants share an ability to store water in their tissues, which allows them to survive in arid climates. Many cacti come from the desert, but some are from jungle environments and need more moisture and less direct sunlight. Many cacti have sharp spines or bristles; some are covered with woolly hairs, such as old man cactus here. Others, such as Christmas and Easter cactus, have neither. The plants can take the form of globes or barrels or cylinders. Some are upright and branched, and others are collections of flattened or rounded or jointed stems. The diversity of sizes and shapes is vast.

Cactus flowers are quite beautiful, with a satiny sheen, and come in a host of warm colors—rich reds, brilliant magentas, softer pinks and salmons, glowing orange, a range of yellows, buff, and white.

Potting Mix: Use a well-drained cactus mix of equal parts potting soil and sharp (builder's) sand, or a mix that includes some compost and small pebbles or fine gravel as well.

Temperature range: A range of 60 to 85°F suits many cacti. Good air circulation is important.

Light: A bright, sunny window with a southern or western exposure is best for desert cacti.

Moisture: Let the potting mix dry out. Then water well. Do not overwater.

Fertilizing: Feed in spring and then every three months during active growth with all-purpose or high-phosphorus fertilizer.

Other care: A winter rest is essential for many cacti to bloom. For this, move the plant to a cool, bright location and do not fertilize. Water only when the soil dries out and the plant begins to shrivel. As days lengthen in spring, water and fertilize. Then water as needed to keep the soil just barely moist.

Repot a cactus when the pot becomes overcrowded. Start new plants from seed or by division of offsets (page 19).

FACT

All cacti are succulents, but not all succulents are cacti. Every true cactus has an areole, or spine cushion—a kind of pore found at nodes on the stems from which spines, hairs, or leaves grow.

Chinese evergreen (*Aglaonema*)

This foolproof foliage plant is perfect for dimly lit rooms without a sunny window. It has oblong, pointed leaves that may be plain green, or mottled and streaked in various combinations of light green, dark green, gray-green, silver, and cream. It grows about 2½ feet tall.

Potting mix: All-purpose potting mix.

Temperature: Temperatures of 65 to 80°F are fine, but easily tolerates 5 to 10 degrees warmer or cooler.

Light: Moderate to low light, no direct sun.

Moisture: Prefers moist soil and plenty of humidity, but it's a tough plant that endures with less. Water when the soil dries below the surface, but do not overwater. A bathroom with a bright window is a good location. Or place the plant on a pebble tray, or mist it often.

Other care: Chinese evergreen needs little care and can tolerate neglect. Remove any old, dried leaves and repot when the plant crowds its pot. Start new plants from stem (cane) cuttings, described on page 18.

HELPFUL TIP

To start new Chinese evergreens, cut off a stem and cut into 2-inch pieces. Each piece that has a scar where a leaf used to be can be planted horizontally an inch deep in moist potting mix to root.

Dumbcane (*Dieffenbachia*)

This handsome foliage plant can withstand neglect, and offers large leaves in different combinations of green, creamy white, and yellow. Dumbcane's sturdy canelike stems can grow to 6 feet, but many newer varieties stay under 3 feet. Dumbcane is extremely easy to grow and can withstand some neglect.

Potting mix: All-purpose potting mix.

Temperature: A range of 60 to 75°F is ideal, but plants adapt to cooler and warmer temperatures.

Light: Bright to moderate light, no direct sun. May sunburn in a south window.

Moisture: Evenly moist, but not soggy; let soil dry slightly before watering. Appreciates humidity but accepts average household levels. Mist in winter.

Fertilizing: Feed monthly in summer, less often in winter.

Other care: Needs little care. Clean leaves with a damp cloth. Remove dried leaves. Repot only when pot is crowded. Start new plants by air layering (pages 20-21) or stem cuttings (page 18).

HELPFUL TIP

A warning about dumbcane (and the reason for its name): Keep the plant away from small children and curious pets because ingesting its leaves or stems causes painful swelling of the mouth.

Dracaena

Rainbow dracaena

Dragon Tree (*Dracaena marginata*)

Dracaena — some variegated dracaenas

Dracaenas are some of the best houseplants. They're versatile and easy to grow, and look good with different decor styles. Dragon tree (*Dracaena marginata*) has an upright, stiff central stem and narrow, pointed green leaves edged in red; one variety has leaves striped in cream and red. Corn plant (*Dracaena massangeana*) has a thicker, woodier, canelike stem. Its leaves are long and pointed—shaped like the leaves of true corn plants—with white or yellow stripes down the center. There's also a maroon-and-green-leaved variety. Varieties of *Dracaena deremensis* have striped leaves ('Janet Craig' as shown), and the leaves of the variety Warneckii are striped in both light and dark green. Dracaenas can grow to 5 feet high or more over time. All of them are easy-care, adaptable houseplants.

Potting mix: Any well-drained, all-purpose potting mix. Drainage is important; the roots will rot in soggy soil.

Temperature: A range of 60 to 75°F is ideal, but plants are adaptable.

Light: Bright to moderate light, no direct sun. Eastern or western exposures, or a bright northern window.

Moisture: Evenly moist but not wet; let soil dry a bit between waterings. Likes humidity, but does fine at average household levels.

Fertilizing: Feed once a month with all-purpose fertilizer.

Other care: Repot only when crowded. Wipe the leaves with damp cloth occasionally to clean them. Start new plants by air layering (pages 20–21) or stem cuttings (page 18).

Lucky Bamboo

Lucky bamboo, that intriguingly twisted plant seen in shops everywhere, often growing in water, isn't a bamboo at all. It's a dracaena. Although the plant will grow for a time in just water, it'll do better planted in soil. If you want to keep yours for a long time, plant it in well-drained, all-purpose potting mix and keep it evenly moist.

To ensure that the stem keeps twisting and turning, set the plant some distance from a bright window and let it grow toward the light. Hang a weight on the stem to keep it from growing vertically. When it has grown in one direction, turn it around so it will again have to reach for the light.

Ferns — Lacy maidenhair fern

Ferns have been household favorites since Victorian days, and they look just as fresh and lovely today. Their graceful fronds soften hard lines of furniture and architecture, and add a textural contrast to smooth surfaces.

Ferns

Button fern

Ferns come from different plant families, but what they share is that none of them bears flowers. They reproduce by means of spores instead of seeds. Their leaves, called fronds, can be divided into leaflets, and many have a delicate, lacy appearance.

The graceful maidenhair fern (*Adiantum*) has light green, fan-shaped leaflets. Best known is the Boston fern (*Nephrolepis*), a vigorous hanging basket plant with divided narrow leaflets; it can grow quite big over time and fill an entire window. Button fern (*Pellaea*) has round leaflets on slender stems. Bird's nest fern (*Asplenium*), page 8, has long, narrow, undivided leaves with ruffled edges and an open center reminiscent of a bird's nest. The intriguing rabbit's foot fern (*Davallia*) has lacy, divided fronds and fuzzy beige rhizomes that creep along on top of the soil.

Potting mix: Most ferns grow best in a rich potting mix that contains a lot of organic matter and combines potting soil with compost and sharp sand. For ferns in hanging baskets, add fir bark chips to the soil.

Temperature: Average household temperatures of 60 to 75°F are best. Keep out of cold drafts.

Light: Moderate light from northern or eastern exposure; no direct sun.

Moisture: Most ferns prefer even moisture, but rabbit's foot fern likes to dry a bit between thorough waterings. Ferns appreciate humidity; place them on a pebble tray or keep them in a bathroom if there's enough light.

Fertilizing: Feed monthly with a mild, all-purpose liquid fertilizer, diluted to half strength. Don't overfeed, or the fronds will turn brown.

Other care: Remove any old, yellowing fronds by cutting them off at the base. Repot when the plant becomes crowded.

INTERESTING FACT

Ferns reproduce by spores, not seeds. A spore geminates to produce a fan-shaped prothallus, which contains male and female reproductive organs that in turn produce the new fern.

Fig (*Ficus*)

Ornamental fig trees have great presence in a room. Best-known is weeping fig (*Ficus benjamina*). It has graceful, glossy green leaves whose tips point downward. In addition to the green-leaved species form, there's also a variety with elegant foliage combining green and creamy yellow. Some weeping figs have decorative braided trunks. The trees can grow to 5 feet or more.

Braided fig

Potting mix: Any well-drained potting mix.
Temperature: A range of 60 to 80°F is perfect. Keep away from drafts and cold air.

Light: Prefers bright to moderate light from an east or west window. No direct sun.

Moisture: Let soil dry slightly between waterings. Mist twice daily or place the pot on a pebble tray. Otherwise easy to grow.

Fertilizing: Feed monthly with all-purpose fertilizer.

Other care: Don't repot weeping fig unless it completely fills the pot—it prefers to be undisturbed. Make new plants by air layering (pages 20-21) when the stem has grown too long.

HELPFUL TIP

Weeping fig is notorious for dropping its leaves as soon as you get it home, caused by dry air. So if your fig defoliates, give it humidity. New leaves will grow when the humidity rises.

Fittonia (or Mosaic) plants

This sweet little foliage plant also goes by the name of mosaic plant, and it's easy to see why. Its dark green, oval leaves are veined in reddish pink or white, tracing a pattern of tiny blocks across the leaves. It's a delightful, compact plant for a north windowsill.

Fittonia is easy to grow and doesn't need lots of light or water. Plant in a pot or hanging basket.

Individual flowers last only about a day before falling.

Potting mix: Rich, humusy potting mix containing some compost.

Temperature: Temperatures between 62 and 75° F are ideal.

Light: Low light from a north or east window.

Moisture: Let the soil dry out just slightly between waterings. Appreciates humidity; mist twice a day or place on a pebble tray.

Fertilizing: Feed monthly while in active growth with mild, all-purpose fertilizer.

Other care: Pinch back stem tips regularly to keep plant compact and bushy. Repot when plant begins to look crowded—it doesn't like to be potbound. In winter, to let the plant rest, stop fertilizing, move plant to a cool room, and cut back on watering but don't let the soil completely dry out. Make more plants by taking stem tip cuttings in spring (page 18).

HELPFUL TIP

Fittonia is a terrific plant for a terrarium—it loves the humid environment.

Gold Dust Plant *(Aucuba)*

This perfectly named plant has dark green leaves that look like they've been sprinkled with gold dust—they're splotched and speckled with yellow. It makes a fine houseplant.

Potting mix: All-purpose potting mix with very good drainage.

Temperature: Generally thrives in a range of 60 to 80°F. It appreciates a nighttime drop in temperature of about 10 degrees.

Light: Likes bright light from an east or west window, but not direct sun.

Moisture: This plant does not like wet feet. Let the soil dry somewhat between waterings, and be sure to empty the saucer underneath the pot after watering.

Fertilizer: Feed once a month during the growing season with a mild all-purpose fertilizer, or every three months with a stronger formula.

Other care: Prune in spring to keep plant compact and improve its shape. Gold dust plant likes a winter rest; gradually decrease watering, but don't let the soil completely dry out. Move plant to a cool room and stop fertilizing. Start new plants from stem tip cuttings in spring.

Gold dust's cousin Japanese laurel 'Borealis' is a very cold-hardy shrub.

Guzmania Bromeliad

Also known as bromeliads, these pineapple relatives add a contemporary accent to a room. The smooth, stiff leaves resemble a frozen green fountain 1½ to 2 feet high. In late winter, a stalk of tiny white flowers surrounded by bright red, orange, or pink bracts arises from the center of the plant. These bracts are actually modified leaves that look like flowers and stay colorful for months.

Colorful bract options

Potting mix: A half-and-half mix of potting soil and fine-grade fir bark, with some perlite or sharp builder's sand added.

Temperature: 60 to 80°F is a good range. Needs good air circulation, but keep out of drafts.

Light: Moderate light but no direct sun. An east window with a sheer curtain is ideal.

Moisture: Keep soil evenly moist but not soggy. Mist daily or set pot on a pebble tray to boost humidity.

Fertilizing: Needs little fertilizer. You may give some all-purpose fertilizer twice yearly, but don't spray the foliage with a liquid fertilizer.

Other care: Guzmania blooms long, but dies when it finishes blooming. To create new plants, remove offsets from the mother plant and pot in separate containers (pages16-17).

HELPFUL TIP

Guzmania's overlapping leaves form a cup in the plant's center. When not blooming, fill the cup with water in addition to keeping the soil moist.

Ivy (*Hedera*)

Variegated ivy

There are lots of pretty varieties, all tough, easy-to-grow houseplants. Plant ivy in a hanging basket and let its stems trail, or train it to climb a trellis in a pot. Ivies are also attractive accent plants for tabletops or countertops.

English ivy (*Hedera helix*) is the most common species, and there are many types, from miniatures with petite leaves to larger forms, in plain green or edged or mottled with creamy white or yellow. All of them have pointed leaves divided into three lobes.

Ivy 'Adam's Choice'

Potting mix: All-purpose potting mix

Temperature: Tolerates a range from 50 to 80°F or more.

Light: Bright light from any exposure. Variegated (two-colored) types like a few hours of direct sun a day.

Moisture: Prefers evenly moist soil, tolerates drier conditions.

Fertilizing: Feed bimonthly with all-purpose fertilizer.

Other care: Remove browning leaves. To keep plants full and bushy, prune the stems in spring. Repot whenever plants seem crowded. Start new plants from stem tip cuttings (page 18).

HELPFUL TIP

Ivy can grow aerial roots along its stems that enable it to climb a bark slab or a moss-covered totem pole.

Jade plant (*Crassula*)

Being washed after wintering indoors, this jade shrub is actually three plants, each started from an individual leaf.

This popular shrub grows slowly to 3 feet, eventually looking like a miniature tree. It's long lived and very easy to grow and propagate from leaf cuttings The round, glossy leaves are thick and fleshy and can store water. If your jade plant gets enough light, you'll be rewarded with clusters of small white flowers.

Potting mix: Well-drained, all-purpose potting mix.

Temperature: Cool to average temperatures, 55 to 75°F.

Light: Bright indirect light from an east or west window. May sunburn in direct sun.

Moisture: Overwatering will kill a jade plant. Keep the soil on the dry side, never soggy.

Fertilizing: Feed bimonthly with all-purpose fertilizer.

Other care: Prefers to be potbound, so don't repot until really crowded. Remove leaves that dry out or drop.

The easiest way to start new jade plants is to pick off a leaf and stick it in a pot of moist potting mix to root, resulting in young shoots like these in less than six months.

Moth orchid (*Phalaenopsis*)

Moth orchid

The perfect orchid for beginners and a wonderful, adaptable houseplant, the moth orchid is pure delight. Its lovely flowers really do look like moths or butterflies, and you can enjoy them in a host of colors: white, pink, lavender, yellow, yellow-green, some with contrasting spots, stripes, or bars on the petals and others with a contrasting lip. When the plants bloom they produce a tall, arching stem with a series of buds that open in succession and then stay in bloom for months. There are literally thousands of moth orchid hybrids, and when you try one you might just find yourself bitten by the orchid bug.

Use twist ties, as shown, to attach stem to stake.

Potting mix: Plant moth orchid in a pot of medium-grade fir bark, or a mix of fir bark and chopped tree-fern fiber.

Temperature: Prefers temperatures ranging from 60 to 85°F. Good air circulation is important, but keep the plant out of cold drafts.

Light: Bright light with no direct sun is best. In an east window, shield the plant from midday sun with a sheer curtain.

Moisture: Keep evenly moist year-round.

Fertilizing: Feed every three weeks with an orchid fertilizer or all-purpose liquid food, or give quarter-strength feedings every time you water.

Other care: Repot plants in fresh fir-bark mix when the plant crowds the pot or when the growing medium deteriorates, about every 12 to 18 months. Remove flowers when they fade, but don't cut down the stem right away; it may send out sideshoots and bloom again.

HELPFUL TIP

Orchid flowers may be as small as 1/16 of an inch across or a broad as 10 inches. The blossoms are intricately constructed and very highly evolved to attract pollinators. There are orchids that resemble pansies and tulips, dancing ballerinas, starfish, spiders and, of course, moths.

Palms Bamboo palm

Palms Chinese fan palm

In summer, move your palm tree out to a shady corner on your deck or patio. Set a lounge chair next to it and put your feet up and you'll feel like you're vacationing on your own little tropical island.

There are many kinds of palms, and they've gone in and out of style as houseplants since the 1800s. They're readily available now, and if you buy one you'll probably have it for years. Bamboo palm (*Chamaedorea erumpens*) is a classic-looking palm with big, arching fronds divided into lots of long, pointed segments. Bamboo palm can reach 5 feet indoors. Another excellent palm for indoor growing, with a very different look, is the Chinese fan palm (*Licuala grandis*). This elegant plant will grow slowly to about 4 feet high, with fan-shaped, pleated leaves of glossy medium green.

You can use palms in all sorts of ways. Because they don't need direct sun, you can place them in a bright corner to fill the space, or behind a sofa. Try a palm in the kitchen or in a roomy bathroom.

Potting mix: Any well-drained all-purpose potting mix.

Temperature: Palms thrive in moderate temperatures of about 65 to 75°F.

Light: Provide moderate light, but no direct sun; an east window covered by a sheer curtain is ideal.

Moisture: Keep soil evenly moist in summer and a bit drier during winter. The tips of the fronds may turn brown if humidity is too low, so mist your palm daily if you can, or place it on a pebble tray.

Fertilizing: Feed every other month with all-purpose fertilizer, or monthly with a half-strength liquid fertilizer. Cut back fertilizer in winter.

Other care: Palms grow slowly and don't mind being potbound, so you won't need to repot them very often, only when they become quite crowded.

TIP

Palms are important in the tropics. They supply food (such as dates and coconuts), fibers for ropes and mats, and livestock feed. You can use coir fiber from coconut palms to lighten potting mixes for houseplants.

Peace lily (*Spathiphyllum*)

Peace lily will grow almost anywhere, whether in low light, on a table or countertop, or atop a file cabinet under fluorescent lights. If you water it, it'll bloom. The glossy, deep green leaves rise on long, slender stems in a loose clump. One variety has leaves splashed and mottled with white. The white flowers appear in spring. They have a single hood-shaped "petal" called a spathe, wrapped around a columnar spadix. With just a bit of care, peace lily will live for years.

Potting mix: Well-drained all-purpose mix.

Temperature: Tolerates a wide range, from 60 to 85°F.

Light: Moderate to low light, no direct sun.

Moisture: Can survive in dry soil, but for flowers keep soil evenly moist. Let soil dry somewhat in winter, when plant likes to rest. Loves humidity but can handle less. To make it really happy, set it on a pebble tray or place in a bathroom that gets steamed up daily.

Fertilizer: Feed bimonthly with all-purpose fertilizer. Cut back on feeding in winter.

Other care: For best growth, scrape some soil from the top of the root ball in spring and add fresh potting mix. Repot when the roots fill most of the pot. Start new plants by division (page 19).

INTERESTING FACT

Peace lily is related to taro, an important food in parts of the tropics.

Peperomia

Peperomias perform beautifully in hanging baskets, and they're easy to grow. These sprawling or trailing foliage plants can grow to 3 feet across. They may have shiny; puckered dark green leaves; fleshy dark green leaves with silver bands; or smooth, glossy leaves of dark green or green and cream. For an eye-catching display, group two or three different kinds in the same container.

Peperomia caperata

Potting mix: Soil-based all-purpose potting mix.

Temperature: Range from 60 to 85°F.

Light: Give solid green varieties bright light with no direct sun. Bicolored leaves develop best color with a little sun. Grow them in an east or west window covered by a sheer curtain.

Moisture: Let dry somewhat between waterings because roots will rot in continuously moist soil. Give extra humidity in summer. Mist daily or use a pebble tray.

Fertilizing: Feed bimonthly in summer with all-purpose fertilizer, or monthly with a liquid plant food diluted to half strength. Cut back on feeding in winter.

Other care: Prune when leggy to keep the plant bushy. Repot in fresh potting mix every spring, but peperomia only needs a bigger pot every two or three years. Start new plants from stem tip cuttings (page 18).

INTERESTING FACT

Peperomia is closely related to the plants from which we get peppercorns and kava-kava (a beverage drunk in the Pacific islands).

Philodendron

The traditional trailing philodendron with its glossy, heart-shaped green leaves is a carefree classic. Let it climb a slab of bark in a pot, or let its long stems dangle from a hanging basket. There are other philodendrons, too. The big, dramatic Rojo Congo has large brownish maroon leaves when young, and acquires touches of red when the plant is fully grown. Leaf stems are red, too. The plant grows to 3 feet high, with an upright but spreading form. There are also medium-size philodendrons with large, arrow-shaped leaves. All philodendrons, whatever their size, are easy to grow.

This philodendron was trained to climb a wooden post by means of staples.
(Site: Hollandia Nursery, Garden & Patio, Bethel, CT)

Potting mix: Any well-drained all-purpose potting mix.

Temperature: Typical household temperatures ranging from 60 to 80°F.

Light: Moderate light from east or west window covered with a sheer curtain.

Moisture: Let soil dry out somewhat between waterings. Give more moisture in hot summer weather, less in winter. Don't overwater.

Fertilizing: Feed monthly with all-purpose fertilizer.

Other care: Clean leaves of larger-leaved varieties occasionally with a damp cloth. Start new plants from stem tip cuttings in summer.

HELPFUL TIP

The key to success with philodendrons is not to overwater them, or the roots can rot.

Polka dot plant (*Hypoestes*)

The adorable little polka dot plant is a great choice for a limited space. Its dark green, oval leaves are spotted and splashed with pink, red, or white. The plant grows just a foot tall, and you can plant different colors together for a nice dash of color in a room.

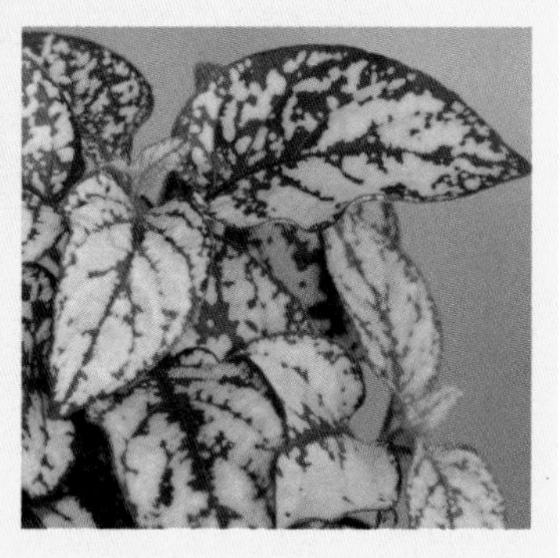

Potting mix: Polka dot plant will grow in all-purpose potting mix, but it really appreciates a richer mix containing more humus.

Temperature: Cool to average temperatures between 55 and 75°F, but adaptable.

Light: Bright light from an east or west window.

Moisture: Evenly moist but never soggy. Appreciates humidity, so mist daily or set plant on a pebble tray.

Fertilizing: Feed monthly in summer with all-purpose fertilizer or every two weeks with a mild liquid fertilizer diluted to half strength.

Other care: Trim back leggy stems in spring. Start new plants from stem tip cuttings (page 18).

HELPFUL TIP

Move polka dot plant outdoors in summer to bring pizzazz to a shady flower bed. It'll look great all summer and loves the shade. Bring indoors in fall when temperatures dip below 50°F at night.

Pothos (*Epipremnum*)

Among the easiest houseplants to grow, pothos give you a lot of bang for the buck. These colorful foliage plants are sometimes mistaken for philodendron because of their heart-shaped leaves. But pothos leaves are marbled in white or golden yellow, whereas philodendron is solid green. Like philodendron, pothos adapts to a range of indoor environments and is entirely undemanding. Its long stems spill out of a hanging basket or climb a trellis or slab of bark in a pot.

Potting mix: All-purpose potting mix.

Temperature: Average household temperatures from 62 to 75°F.

Light: Practically any amount of light from bright to low, though it may burn in direct sun.

Moisture: For optimum growth, keep soil evenly moist, but drier soil won't hurt pothos. Let soil dry between waterings in winter.

Fertilizer: Feed every 2 weeks from spring to fall with all-purpose liquid fertilizer or a higher nitrogen formula. Reduce fertilizer in winter.

Other care: Cut back ends of stems if they get too long, or to promote bushier growth. Repot in fresh potting mix every few years. Start new plants from stem tip cuttings (page 18). They root easily.

HELPFUL TIP

An old-fashioned name for pothos is devil's ivy, perhaps because like other plants in the Aroid Family, pothos leaves contain crystals that irritate the mouth if eaten. It is considered toxic to cats and dogs.

Prayer Plant (*Calathea* and *Maranta*)

Prayer plants have striking, broadly oval leaves with prominent, colorful veins or leaf markings, and they're old favorites among houseplant aficionados. The leaves may be striped with red between the veins, veined in red and patterned in green, lined with cream, splotched with dark brownish green, or light green edged in dark green and flushed with pinkish red. They're eye-catching.

Potting mix: Well-drained, all-purpose or richer, humusy potting mix.

Temperature: 65 and 80°F suit prayer plants; keep out of cold drafts.

Light: Bright light, no direct sun, which can turn leaf tips dry and brown.

Moisture: Evenly moist soil. Mist daily or set pot on a pebble tray.

Fertilizing: Feed bimonthly with mild all-purpose fertilizer.

Other care: Remove any dried-out leaves. Plants like to be potbound, so don't repot them until they become quite crowded. Plants rest in winter. So it's wise to move them to a cooler spot, stop fertilizing, and water only to keep the soil from drying out. Start new plants by division (page 19).

Prayer plants generally grow between 1 and 2 feet high.

INTERESTING FACT

Prayer plants have the interesting habit of closing up their leaves at night, as if they are folding their hands to pray.

Purple Passion Plant (*Gynura*)

Purple passion is a real conversation piece. Its leaves and stems are covered with soft purple hairs, making it a velvety combination of purple and green. Purple passion is not at all fussy. With a little TLC, it will brighten your home for years.

Potting mix: Any all-purpose potting mix.

Temperature: Range of temperatures from 60 to 80°F.

Light: To maintain richest color, give bright to moderate light from an east or west window, with some direct sun.

Moisture: Keep soil evenly moist. Water from the bottom, to avoid getting water on the leaves.

Fertilizing: Feed monthly from spring to fall with a mild, all-purpose fertilizer. Don't spray a foliar fertilizer on the leaves.

Other care: To keep plants compact and bushy, cut back stems when they start to get leggy. Purple passion likes leg room, so repot when roots fill half the space in the pot. The plant likes a winter rest. So cut back on feeding then, and water only enough to keep the soil barely moist. Start new plants from stem tip cuttings in summer (page 18).

HELPFUL TIP

Purple passion plant is sometimes attacked by whiteflies. You'll know if you have them when you gently shake the plant—they'll fly around in a little white cloud. Use insecticidal soap if they strike.

Rubber Plant (*Ficus*)

Rubber plant is a big, bold sculptural plant that says "tropics." It may look like a tree with a single stem, or like a bushy clump of several stems when you buy it. Indoors, it grows 3 feet or more. The leathery leaves are big and paddle shaped, and may be glossy dark green or splotched with pink and cream or light green. The burgundy variety has a reddish tone and red midribs in the leaves when grown in bright enough light. Plants bleed sticky white sap when cut.

Potting mix: All-purpose potting mix.

Temperature: 60 to 85°F

Light: Bright to moderate light from east or west window.

Moisture: Let soil dry somewhat between waterings. Do not overwater, or plant will drop leaves. Mist once or twice daily, or place on pebble tray.

Fertilizing: Feed monthly in spring and summer with all-purpose fertilizer. Don't feed in winter when the plant rests.

Other care: Likes to be potbound, so don't repot until roots fill the pot; repot in spring. Clean leaves with damp cloth occasionally. Air-layer older plants with long bare stems (pages 20-21).

HELPFUL TIP

Rubber trees readily grow toward the light, so turn them weekly to keep them growing straight.

Snake Plant (*Sansevieria*)

Snake Plant (*Sansevieria*)

Snake plant is all about verticality. And neglect. It will grow practically anywhere. Its clean, sculptural line is perfect for a contemporary setting. The plant is a clump of flat, twisting leaves that shoot skyward, and it needs practically no care. It's been grown in people's homes for over 100 years. Its dramatic, thrusting, swordlike form may have inspired another of its nicknames—mother-in-law's tongue.

Sansevieria offers a variety of leaf patterns; they may be dark green banded with yellow, golden-edged with green patterning, a combination of light and dark green, or blue-green edged in white. Plants grow slowly to 2 to 3 feet high.

Potting mix: Any all purpose potting mix.

Temperature: Loves a range of 60 to 85°F but tolerates warmer and cooler temperatures too.

Light: Snake plant thrives in bright light and plenty of sun. Grows in dimmer places, too, but looks its best in good light.

Moisture: Let soil dry before watering. Do not overwater; if the soil stays wet, the leaves will eventually collapse at the soil level.

Fertilizing: Feed monthly or bimonthly with mild all-purpose fertilizer.

Other care: Doesn't need much care. Likes to be potbound; don't repot until it's really crowded. Remove dried or dead leaves. Start new plants from leaf cuttings, as shown here.

To start new snake plants, remove a healthy leaf, cut it into pieces, and insert the pieces into moist potting mix.

Here's how to start new snake plants:

- Cut off a healthy leaf at the base.
- On a clean cutting board, cut the leaf into pieces 2– 2½ inches long.
- Plant the leaf pieces in moist potting mix, pushing them halfway into the soil. Plant top piece with cut-side down. Keep soil moist until roots form. Then transplant the new plants.

Spider Plant (*Chlorophytum*)

Spider Plant (*Chlorophytum*)

A longtime favorite, the spider plant with its arching, green-and-white-striped leaves is ideal for a high shelf or a hanging basket. It's easy to grow and can stand up to some neglect—a good choice for an office or just about any place where it can get a decent amount of light. Spider plant has the rather endearing habit of producing "babies"—little offset plants that it sends out on long, slender runners. You can detach them from the parent plant and pot them up—also a fun project for children.

Potting mix: Any all-purpose potting mix works.

Temperature: Average household temperatures between 60 and 75°F are perfect, but this plant will handle cooler and warmer temperatures.

Light: Spider plant will flourish in bright to moderate light, and will adapt to an unobstructed north window.

Moisture: Provide even moisture, or let the soil dry somewhat between waterings. Anything between wet and bone dry will work. The plant appreciates humidity and would be happy with misting or a pebble tray, but it will tolerate drier air.

Fertilizing: Feed every two or three months with all-purpose fertilizer.

Other care: The plant likes to be potbound, so you won't need to repot until the roots are really crowding the pot. If some leaf tips turn brown, trim them with scissors and try to increase the humidity around the plant. Make new plants by severing babies from the mother plant and potting them up individually.

Each spider plant baby can become a new plant. Cut the baby from its long stem (then cut off the stem at its base and discard it). Set the baby in a small pot of moist potting mix, pushing the bottom gently into the soil. Keep the soil moist until the baby grows roots.

Ti Plant (*Cordyline*)

The Hawaiian ti plant with its pointed, shiny green leaves was all the rage in the 1970s and now it's back, better and more colorful than ever. The ti plant you'll most often see for sale now is a vivid blend of hot pink, cream, and green. It's an eye-catcher, no doubt about it, and a dynamic accent plant, especially in a neutral-colored room.

Potting mix: Well-drained all-purpose potting mix, or a richer, humusy mix.

Temperature: Evenly warm temperatures 62 to 72°F.

Light: Bright light from an east or west window. Direct sun from a southern exposure could burn the leaves.

Moisture: Keep soil evenly moist, but don't worry if soil dries out somewhat between waterings—the plant can take it. Mist daily or place on a pebble tray to boost humidity.

Fertilizing: Feed every 2 or 3 months with all-purpose fertilizer, or monthly with half-strength liquid fertilizer.

Other care: Ti plant doesn't like its roots disturbed and likes to be pot-bound, so repot only when roots completely fill the pot. Promptly remove dried or dead leaves. Clean leaves with a damp cloth. Start new plants from stem cuttings (page 18) or by air layering (pages 20-21).

HELPFUL TIP

The colorfully leaved ti plant is more sensitive than the all-green type. But with good light, and steady moisture and temperatures year-round, the plant will thrive.

Umbrella Plant (*Brassaia* aka *Schefflera*)

This stalwart of shopping-mall thoroughfares is a handsome, easy-to-grow choice for the home. A variegated variety whose green leaves are edged with white has added panache. Umbrella plant brings a lush, tropical note to décor and adapts to a range of indoor environments, growing 4 to 5 feet at home. The arrangement of the oblong leaves around the end of a stem looks something like the ribs of an umbrella and probably inspired the name.

Variegated umbrella plant

Potting mix: All-purpose potting mix.

Temperature: 55 to 75°F; can handle more warmth in summer.

Light: Bright light, no direct sun.

Moisture: Let the soil dry a bit between thorough waterings. Mist daily or set on a pebble tray.

Fertilizing: Feed bimonthly with all-purpose fertilizer that's higher in nitrogen, or monthly with all-purpose fertilizer diluted to half strength.

Other care: Repot when crowded. So the plant can rest in winter, stop feeding and cut back on water. Start new plants from stem cuttings (page 18) or air layering of older plants (page 20-21).

HELPFUL TIP

Your umbrella plant will love a lukewarm shower from time to time. Or, after you've taken a shower and shut off the water, set the plant in the shower and let it luxuriate in the steam.

Vase Plant (*Aechmea*)

Water directly into the "cup."

(Site: Hollandia Nursery, Garden & Patio, Bethel, CT)

Vase Plant (*Aechmea*)

With its bold, stiffly arching leaves, the living vase, or urn, plant looks like a piece of living sculpture. Its dramatic form and clean lines are perfectly suited to a contemporary setting. Vase plant belongs to the pineapple family, and a look at its leaves shows why. Several varieties are on the market. The most familiar urn plant (*Aechmea fasciata*) has silver-frosted leaves and a single, large flower structure made up of tiny blue flowers surrounded by a crown of pink bracts (modified leaves). Another species (*Aechmea chantinii*) has glossy green, stiffly arched leaves and striking reddish pink or orange bracts surrounding the minute blue flowers. Both plants have a "cup" in the center of the plant that holds water. When the plants bloom, the flowers last for months.

Potting mix: Grow vase plant in fine-grade fir bark or a mix of 1 part potting soil, 2 parts fine fir bark, and 1 part sharp (builder's) sand.

Temperature: Moderate, even temperatures around 65 to 70°F are best.

Light: Bright light from a south or east window, but no direct sun. Filter the sun with a sheer curtain.

Moisture: Keep the central cup filled with water in spring and summer, and change the water weekly. Let the potting mix dry out somewhat between waterings. The plant likes humidity, so mist daily or place it on a pebble tray.

Fertilizing: Needs little fertilizer. Apply a small amount of mild, all-purpose fertilizer to the growing medium every few months, but do not spray leaves with liquid fertilizers.

Other care: The plant dies after blooming, though the dying may take as long as two years. Usually vase plant will produce offsets which you can remove and pot up to grow into new plants. The plant likes to rest in fall and winter. During those seasons, stop filling the cup with water, keep the potting mix just barely moist, and do not fertilize.

TIP

One myth that's grown up around vase plant is that enclosing it in a plastic bag with an apple will make it bloom. That doesn't work, unfortunately. Just give it the right growing conditions and be patient.

Wax Plant (*Hoya carnosa*)

The hanging, curly-leaved cultivar is 'Regalis,' also known as Hindu rope plant. At right, Hollandia Garden staff trained this wax plant's stems up a wire support structure.

(Site: Hollandia Nursery, Garden & Patio, Bethel, CT)

Wax Plant (*Hoya carnosa*)

The exotic wax plant, hailing from China, India, and Burma, is a woody vine with glossy, thick, dark green leaves and lovely clusters of star-shaped, waxy, honey-scented flowers that may actually drip sweet nectar. The flowers are white with red centers. There are several other varieties. Wax plant may take a couple of years to bloom after you bring it home because the stems need to be at least 3 feet long before the plant produces flowers. But those flowers are worth the wait, and the leaves are handsome in their own right. You can grow wax plant in a hanging basket or train the long stems to climb a trellis or wind around a circular hoop.

Potting mix: Use an all-purpose potting mix.

Temperature: Household temperatures slightly on the cool side—60 to 70°F—are ideal.

Light: Loving bright light and sun, wax plant does best in a south or east window.

Moisture: Provide enough water to keep the soil evenly moist in spring and summer when the plant blooms. The rest of the year, let the soil become fairly dry between waterings.

Fertilizing: Provide some all-purpose or high-potassium fertilizer once a month in spring and summer, but do not overfeed. Otherwise, the buds may drop off.

Other care: Wax plant blooms best when potbound. After blooming, carefully remove the old flowers or let them drop off naturally. Don't remove the woody stem (called a spur) on which the flowers bloomed because that's where next year's flowers will be produced. Start new plants from stem tip cuttings (page 18).

Wax plant loves sun, but strong midday sun from a south window may be too much for it. If you notice leaf damage in a very sunny window, move the plant or place a sheer curtain over the window.

Index

Aechmea, 60–61
African violets, 24–25
Aglaonema, 30
Air layering, 20–21
Air-purifying plants, 6
Anthurium (*Anthurium*), 26
Areole, 29
Aucuba, 38
Balfour aralia, 27
Bird's nest fern, 8, 35
Boston fern, 35
Bracts, 39
Braided fig, 36
Brassaia, 59
Bromeliad, 39
Button fern, 35
Cacti, 28–29
Calathea, 51
Cephalocereus senilis, 29
Chinese evergreen, 6, 30
Chinese fan palm, 45
Chlorophytum, 56
Christmas cactus, 29
Compost, 11
Cordyline, 58
Corn plant, 6, 33
Crassula, 41
Crown plant, 28
Dieffenbachia, 31
Diseases, 23
Dividing plants, 19
Dracaena deremensis
  'Janet Craig,' 33
Dracaena marginata, 32–33
Dracaena massangeana, 33
Dracaenas, 32–33
Dragon tree, 32–33
Dumbcane, 31
Easter cactus, 29
Electric lights, 9
English ivy, 40
Epipremnum, 50
Ferns
  Bird's nest, 8, 35
  Boston, 35
  Button, 35
  Lacy maidenhair, 34
  Rabbits' foot, 35
Fertilizers, 12–13
Ficus
  Rubber plant, 53
  benjamina, 36
Figs, 36
Fir bark, 11
Fish emulsion, 12
Fittonia, 36
Gold dust plant, 38
Grooming, 16
Guzmania, 39
Gynura, 52
Hedera helix, 40
Hoya carnosa, 62–63
Hollandia Nursery, Garden & Patio, 10, 60, 62
Horticultural oil, 23
Humidity, 15
Insecticidal soap, 23
Ivy, 40
Jade plant, 41
Light, 8
Lucky bamboo, 33
Maidenhair fern, lacy, 34
Maranta, 51
Mealy bugs, 23
Mosaic plant, 37
Mother-in-law's tongue, 55
Moth orchid, 42–43
Nitrogen, 13
Offsets, dividing, 19
Old man cactus, 29
Palms, 44–45
  Bamboo, 44–45
  Chinese fan, 45
Peace lily, 46
Peat moss, 11
Pebbles, 11
Pebble tray, 15, 22
Peperomia, 47
Perlite, 11
Pests, 23
Phalaenopsis, 42–43
Philodendron, 48
Phosphorus, 13
Polka dot plant, 49
Polyscias, 27
Potassium, 13
Pothos, 50
Pot options, 10
Potting mixes, 11
Potting soil, 11
Prayer plant, 51
Propagation, 18
Pruning, 16
Purple passion plant, 5
Rabbit's foot fern, 35
Rainbow dracaena, 32
Repotting, 16–17
Rebutia hybrid, 28
Rubber plant, 53
Saintpaulia, 24–25
Sand, 11
Sansevieria, 54–55
Scale, 23
Schefflera, 59
Snake plant, 54–55
Spathiphyllum, 46
Spider mites, 23
Spider plant, 56–57
Stakes and supports, 2
Stem cuttings, 18
Stem tip cuttings, 18
Tail flower, 26
Ti plant, 58
Tools, 22
Toughest plants, 6
Umbrella plant, 59
Urn plant, 60
Vase plant, 60–61
Vermiculite, 11
Watering, 14
Watering can, 22
Wax plant, 62–63
Weeping fig, 36

Houseplants for All Season

Houseplants are a beautiful addition to any room or office. They brighten the space we live in. From luscious foliage plants; hanging baskets, cacti and succulents; to flowering pot plants including exotics such as bromeliads and orchids; let our easy-to-follow guide, full of helpful tips, help you select and care for the plants which are right for you.

Anne Halpin is the author of 17 books, including *Homescaping: Designing Your Landscape to Match Your Home, Seascape Gardening, The Horticulture Gardener's Desk Reference*. She has written articles for *VOX, The Southampton Press, Horticulture, Country Gardens,* and *Country Home* magazines, and others. In addition to her publishing activities, Anne is a professional gardener, caring for private gardens on Long Island.

TYPHOON
MEDIA CORPORATION

$3.95 U.S./$4.95 Can.
ISBN 13: 9781600814440
ISBN 10: 1600814441